MORAL SLOTH

MORAL SLOTH

NICK ASCROFT

VICTORIA UNIVERSITY PRESS

VICTORIA UNIVERSITY PRESS
Victoria University of Wellington
PO Box 600 Wellington
vup.victoria.ac.nz

First published 2019

A catalogue record is available at the National Library of New Zealand

ISBN 9781776562398

Printed by Blue Star, Wellington

Contents

i. Publicly Disgraced

Five Ways I Would End a Sonnet on Shelley's Cremation

So Mary looked around, suppressed a cough.
Lord Byron lit his fag and tottered off.

**

And when before St Pete the Bysshe appeared,
still drunk on brine, he pulled at Peter's beard.
What larks, said he, I find your hedge a hairy'un.
But God was neither dead nor vegetarian.

**

  In Italy the law's a florin lean:
them who dies by sea must quarantine
  and burn on sand afar of foreign green.

**

He either drowned or was assassinated,
or was a little soon, alas, cremated.

**

The fire like a tide washed over him,
till like the sea his bones were black and grim.
The funeral done, we had a lovely swim.

Wellington Zoo 44 Rewritten

after David Beach

The zoo staff comforted the boy's distraught
progenitors (albeit while restraining
them). The sign was clear. The kid was caught:
there really wasn't any point complaining.
'If you feed the animals you will
be fed to them.' A meagre dish for these
already ill-served beasts perhaps, but still
the regulation's beneficiaries
magnanimously pawed the air and roared
consent. The viewing deck was packed. We beamed:
morale among the lions was restored.
They swung him up towards the glass. He screamed,
'I'll never feed an animal again!'
A quite transparent lie, in the event.

Reflections on Emptiness, Celebrity and Agency, Having Visited Patrick Pound's Hall of Mirrors

i. The Queen Should Take Things Easy

The doctors-to-royalty beckoned:
'Queen Lizzie Regina II,
you ought to head bedward,'
they said. (She'd had Edward.)
Best to rest these elite medics reckoned.

ii. Miss Hearst Had Been Taken to Stanford for Psychiatric Tests

Patty Hearst is her own palindrome:

the bland celebrity mirroring her shadow
and the shadow attached at the shoes again

to the heiress pardoned,
and a paper-doll chain of John Waters cameos,
folding her storied life over and over.

Her father sold newspapers from without
and she from within.
Patty Hearst is driven into court
and the car reverses back out again

towards the mental hospital.
Psychiatrists say she is not the curator of her life.
The Symbionese Liberation Army

had taken the small pieces
and rearranged them back to front.

If she wanted to rob the bank

it was just the echo of their want of her
to want to.

It's a line no one likes.
Desire is our own.
We have will

and we choose to exercise it for good or for crookery.
We are not products of our abduction.
We are not made into zombies of our legal selves
by degradation and torment.

If that were true the jails of the world would be full
of innocents.
But look in their eyes.
We have jails because evil is quantifiable and
not simply an image projected onto others

of our desire to accuse
and loft ourselves up.
There are hard lines to maintain
lest our moral bedrock liquefy.
We have free will.
We are not walking out the paces

of a life shaped ahead of time for us.
Desire is our own.

Though tugged at by advertising

and the dubious politics of our associates,
we are the authors of our choices.

I am being ironic,
saying one thing and meaning the antithesis.
This is candour, irony's awful inverse.

We are spiders,
singing pieties as we trawl for victims.

We apologise, backlighting our sins as virtue.

This poem is the smoke and mirror
of a counterfeit apologist,

framing itself,
believing itself good.
Its rhetoric is designed to protect it.

Patty Hearst's captors were leftist radicals, feminists,
exposing her to sexual freedom.

We cry arachnid tears,

gesticulating with the front four legs
our solidarity and grief,

while the back four are drawn on by each strand.
Just one slick strand, what harm is that?
The women must have protected her,
the prosecution says.
Their ideology's angelic heart must have held to that.
It must have been internally consistent

in some throwback Victorian necessity,
even as they kept her blindfolded
in a broom cupboard.
The snare's larger symmetry is unknown
to the thing spinning it.

It is unaware even of itself.
Patty Hearst robbed the bank with glee,
stole a car with charm.
Charm and glee cannot be the products

of a washed brain.
We own our charm and glee.
The court is in two minds,

like a Siamese twin.
It regurgitates the required doublespeak:

guilty.

Guilty so as not to be reflected back
through newspapers and precedent

that we fall neatly into our shadows.
There is a double standard for the rich,
but the opposite of which you think.

John Wayne cries brainwashing.
John Wayne, hater of the flimsy kissy boys.
The man of will,
the man for whom manliness was will itself

cries the wateriness of the brain.
Her crime was to be a woman.
To not be John Wayne's self-projection.

To be rich.
Her crime was to be a photograph,

and its negative.

*iii. Ronald Reagan Emphasises a Point While Talking to Newsmen
    in Sacramento Today*

Columnist Drew Pearson lied.
Today Ronald Reagan denied
a homosexual ring
in nor east nor west wing
was at all operating inside.

What to Avoid Calling My Next Poetry Collection

You're Going to Need a Big Old Dictionary
What to Expectorate When Your Expectorating
Fanny Pack of Wolves
Words Good
Dry, Slow, Grinding, Unremitting, Desolate, Endless

Dwang Nibbler
Full Metal Jean Shorts
You Don't Have Time for This
Treat Your Own Neck
Fey Canoes

Your Haircut Looks Like a Pauper's Grave
Your Pauper's Grave Is a Bit Ooh-Look-at-Me
Unstapleshuttable
People Who Bought This Also Bought Pornography
Smellybutton

I Preferred His Early Funny Poems
Just Thoughts Really
Limericks for Pubic Baldness
Charge Conjugation Parity Symmetry Violation for Dummies
Hang on, Nobody Wang Chung a Second

Impervious to Criticism
Found Poems of Financial Regulation
Away with Words
Fighting Fire with Fire Extinguishers
There Was an Old Lady from Lucknow

Most Eligible Lecturer
You People
Once Were Wordier
Cry Me ¡*Arriba*!
What to Ejaculate When You're Ejaculating

Suckle on My Verse Teats
Emilio Estevez
10 Child Abduction Fails #3 Is Hilarious
Your Feet Honk Like Tofurkey
Wheeeeeeeee!

Three Questions for a Job Interview

Do you have a birth story, which is to say, your mother's labour, was it a terrifying adventure, and were there forceps?

When you were young and idealistic, is this how you saw your future: the drudgery, repetition and underutilisation of your capacities?

Do you actively dread death, or do you repress all thoughts of it, or are you at peace with the idea of your own cessation?

ii. Loathed for their Cowardice

Gone Mad

Health and safety gone mad.

Disease and hazard gone mad.

'Health and safety gone mad' gone mad.

Healthy dislike of Baby Boomers gone mad.

Housing prices gone mad.

Interest rates threatening to spiral out of control but remaining at a
plateau gone mad.

Estate agents gone mad.

I'm stuck in an elevator with three of them with only a safety pin
and malice aforethought gone mad.

Zika outbreak spreading like wildfire gone mad.

Zika outbreak media announcements of successful containment
gone mad.

The alt-right gone mad.

The alt-mad gone right gone mad.

The countryside, the city, the coast, the island off the coast gone mad.

The island descending under rising sea levels with ice caps going,
going, gone mad.

The nanny state gone mad.

Europe gone mad.

The Middle East gone mad.

Turkey straddling both while elbowing itself in the vagina gone mad.

The Philippines gone mad.

The otherwise calm and dispassionate alpine nation of Switzerland
gone mad.

The fledgling autonomous region of Rojava *not yet gone mad*.

Self-righteous moralising gone mad.

Scepticism fatigue gone mad.

Shrill liberal echo chambers gone mad.

The internet and its sequel, the dark internet rises, gone mad.

The fake-news-bot generators gone mad.

The Al Jazeera autocue gone mad.

Some talking headshot gone off on one gone mad.

Gone Daddy Gone diddy doo-wah diddy bada bing bada bang
gone mad.

Mod cons gone mad.

Maud Gonne gone mad.

The Maud Gonne Band gone mad.

The Michael Jackson album *Bad* gone mad.

The satirical magazine from the 1980s *Cracked* gone mad.

PC gone mad.

PCP gone mad.

CCCP gone mad.

Pea soup gone mad.

Healthy pee is not sea green gone mad,

but gone girls have gone with the wind gone mad.

Schizophrenic disassociative copralalia gone mad.

Humanity, one day everywhere like vermin, and the next, gone:
mad!

Psalm Accompanied by Hipster Cacophony

Thou shineth as does spilt petroleum;
You gleam like freshly mopped linoleum.
O Thou who never frets or gets despondent
who riseth like a yawn but holdeth back it
– like unto a foreign correspondent –
withstand we beg our lamentation's racket.

Hail Him with tropes designed to sell
a psalm, an antithetic parallel
say: good folk read, the ill have aerials.
Extol Him pure or with occult bloodletting,
or by repurposing materials
intended for a wholly different setting.

O praise Him on the tuba and euphonium.
O praise Him Browningesque and/or Byronian.

Selfie, Dumfries, 1998

The Christmas Eve that twinkled green and red
within my lovesick eyes withstood the bruise
at arm's length of the flash. I made a bed
on Burns's grave and let the drizzle muse
at middle-aged colonial conceits,
the kind my bones were weathering to suit
in other drunken far and future streets,
the winter less Dickensian and cute.
I rose and moped the churchyard in a blank,
until that emptied out and nothing pulled
me back down to the pub where nothing drank
its empty glass. The negative still spooled
unpainted in its roll was to have been
a metaphor, was to have meant to mean.

Self-Planting of Evidence

I vacillate between the expedient and the
fastidious: write it on the corner of a nearby receipt
or go and fetch a clean piece of paper and welcome
the ease of the experience.
I use a pentacle instead of an asterisk

when I make bullet lists in pen.
I appreciate the madness of living and its balance of wild risks,
but without their wildness and imaginable danger the thing
would be worse.
True I suspect for lions and cheetahs, our old cousins and

acquaintances of the savannah. Things to avoid meet
emotions of deterrent
and attractors thrill, the self-abuse of decision-making.
Their fear of missing the mark on the
back of the hartebeest's leg feels awful, and

the delight of the kill drags them around
like greyhounds. How does it feel? No
different to yourself, the wordless chemical torture
of the inner awareness.
It's only fear that makes me hide the truth.

No More Experimental Poetry

The cacophony of salt
bristling down from unheaven,
the little chariotborne oraclemongers,
eyes of hellfire,

the night's thinking we sweat awake out of,
all of the shambling poor,
bowing channelled fiddles of their dead,
and the motey

morality hanging in its air

from the beaten mat
of my figment, my imagined gist

of an argument for,
they all descend
below the neckwear, and my shoulders
huff back up into it.

To say there is no ought is to be
not naive but
uninsured against those who disagree,
including your own self-perjuring.

Late Night Horror

I missed the bus by about 25 seconds,
looked up, chased after it, and jogged to
a stop. The next one was in maybe
half an hour. I came to no action point or
managerial decision as such. I was just
walking up the hill in the dark.
After 15 minutes I had passed the third

stop, and something in me, some
mathematical subsection, suggested I
was better off to wait there.
That was when the first guy screamed
at me out his window.
Before television we'd had the elderly.
Some late genetic compulsion had them

extemporising on the long and varied
subject matter they'd taken in, not
on purpose, passive to it, but now with the
urge to tell everyone the details.
We looked around for an entertainment suite,
there was none, so we listened in.
There were recurring themes and

characters. Tragedy and dramedy and
light car-crash tragicomic reality, and
informercials – I don't know, for faith,
planning ahead, conservatism – and
late night horror. Sometimes they'd go

into a holding pattern and you'd have
to whack them on the side.

I was still at the bus stop. The mathematics
in me hadn't said anything.
No one else had harassed me, even though
I was whispering to myself. No one
else had leant out their window and
howled some great inner necessity.
The timetable agreed that there was half

an hour between buses and it was only the
second to last I was waiting on.
My phone battery expired. Another
car slowed to lurch around the hairpin
just up from me. We were now – or would've
been – the elderly, and felt the urge to
broadcast and expound, but to no one.

iii. Loathed for the Bravery
to Speak Unfashionable Truths

The Plotz

Phlegmatic, I'm not one to plotz or wax
nostalgic for a life that could've been.
I bumble forward, shuffling in my tracks
to work and back again. The kitchen's clean.
I use Excel to calculate Kate's tax.
I had once dreamt I'd be a libertine,
admired for simile and malaprop.
The 90s raised me up then let me drop.

Back then, each anecdote would cost you corkage,
my poems swigged on flasks, were furious
and hot with psychedelic flash and squawkage.
I blazed, affectedly bi-curious.
These days I just complain about the mortgage,
all other matters somehow spurious
and flat. I spend the evening sudsing plates
and pots, in fear of rising interest rates.

Not one to plotz, I'm private, careful, flaccid.
How did I change? One moment I wear blouses,
vinyl shoes, I'm pulverised on acid,
the next I'm at the bank discussing houses
or circling with a whiteboard marker 'hazard
class', a tucked-in shirt with belted trousers.
I want to understand, to tweeze this tuft.
Did I grow up? Or was my brightness snuffed?

Before I went under a nom de plume,
before the bank had made a covenant
with me to slavishly add commas to
abhorrent documents for subsequent
emolument, I lived in Oamaru.
(I still took money from the government,
the dole.) And from that opposite of Eden,
I drag the band with me down to Dunedin.

I trip the halls like velvet under my
beret, a lip-stuck elf with pointed toes.
I study language, thought, but wonder why,
in chief, so few enjoy my gigs, or prose.
A typically blind-spotted blunder: I'm
unchanged it seems. Less fresh of gill, less rosy
eyed, perhaps, but so alike in fact
of taste and dreams. My foibles are intact

at least. The years gallumph like this. I shake
songwriting off and go for verse. They're kinder,
literary types. I'd tried to break
our demo to a label not inclined to
it. Pete from Snapper said we're a mistake.
I graduate, am single (dumped), and find a
bookshop gig. It's 1998.
I chase a girl, and demonstrate I'm straight

by kissing boys just to ensure we will
avoid the sin of overegging hetero.
My gender freedom is sartorial.
Free too from time, I dress embracing retro.

London is more dictatorial.
It frowns. And though years pass before I let go,
it schools me how to look more apropos,
to come across more man than man-mango.

The movie I'd self-finance of my life
(the casting option either Aquaman
or Jesse Eisenberg – and here my wife
can roll her eyeballs) would compact a span
of years into a weekend on a knife-
edge. Sleeping at a bus stop backward, fanned
around my bag, cold in PVC,
I doze, am homeless, terrified, but free.

Above, the stars are smothered by the smog.
I'm outside Heathrow, stuck until the Tubes
resume. They treat a person like a dog.
To bed, they say, till six. Go to your rooms,
you Londoners. The pubs lock up the grog.
But airports, they're all hours, one presumes?
Two coppers sweeping shake their heads, say no.
I make it through the night outside, then go.

I stay with Andy's friends near Glastonbury.
I have no job and live on money sponged
from Kim, back home, who'd said if drastically
required I could use her card – I lunged –
and cash from Mum as well, left spastically
behind in Wimbledon. Their flat's implunged
in odour, but they offer me a niche
to kip in, and tobacco with hashish.

The two are always smoked together, all
day long and every day by him in whom
I see a British doppelgänger, tall
and slim, long hair. It's not the constant fume
emitted from his lips that splits us, or will
once I partake. It's that he bears a gloom.
That's Britain, and its thrashing underclass.
He takes a kicking in an underpass.

The nights unfold with dramas of the poor.
A day's work picking peas from yellow turf.
We mark the solstice drumming on the Tor.
At Argos, blag a tent, intending to return
it after camping in the mud before
the policy – 'no questions' – comes to term.
The festival itself is glad, we're gladder
still we stole in with a home-made ladder.

Returning back to Wimbledon, I claw
my horde of traveller's cheques in glee
then crash out in the sticks, a room, well, floor
some kid – the dealer of whose ecstasy
I'd met – extends an open offer for.
This stranger's kind. I rest my neck rent-free.
One sleeps more, if turns less, when in a bed,
but cushions brace my hip and ease my head.

The weeks rotate. I get a ten-hour job,
but till I'm paid, possessing no per diem,
I can't examine ethics like a snob.
I think, 'They're not as hungry', when I see them.

'These tourists shouldn't miss a couple bob,'
and fleece them as they ramble the museum.
That is, the cashier does, when she miscounts
their change. I simply balance the amounts.

Asleep, the kid I stay with moans and keens.
Still dossing every evening in the sticks,
the tube and bus is just within my means
but only once perfecting certain tricks
to keep the Travelcard inside my jeans.
I search under his bed, there's porn, the pix
are strange to me: in each the women flick
their eyes to where above there hangs a dick.

Two times I sleep at Jon's. His place is bleaker:
Paddington, guests not allowed, and stinking.
My presence irks his girlfriend, one Tameka.
I was naive to leave New Zealand thinking
that I'd just stay with Jon, the pleasure seeker.
The cops raid our speakeasy. But a winking
dealer passing sells us . . . *oregano!?*
'Race traitor!' chirrups T like a soprano.

The lowest point before I get a proper
bedsit of my own in Saint John's Wood,
is when I beg Tameka for a Whopper,
and she assents, annoyed to feel she should.
This is the seed. I never want to cop the
look again. And so ends childhood.
The film returns. I'm at the bus stop, cold,
inhaling in short draughts. The credits roll.

I grow I think from this. I learn the scaled
threat of non-conformance. It's no shame
and easier to navigate regaled
as others, smart, domesticated, tame.
Another view is that in fact I've failed
to change a jot. That I remain the same
pretentious fool and cautious pragmatist,
and always was a dry protagonist.

The Mosque Attacks

A certain governmental agency
provisioning the arts suggested in
the aftermath that those invested in
opposing such disgusting vagrancy
of moral intellect should hashtag works
of art or prose on Twitter: '#CreateAroha'.
I looked up from whichever car or bar
I lay slopped out in, tweeting. My knee jerks
at eager-beaver positivity.
I found the notion quite infernal.
I mean, I understood, but some wee kernel
of the 90s in me, given the
controls, yet wary of its influence,
typed – then deleted – '#CreateImpotence'.

Art Is Weak

Conceptual art is not so empty sleeved
and brained. I think of Ai Weiwei's exhibit
spread across the Turbine Hall. Conceived
as interactive, we had to ad-lib it
when, declared a health and safety hazard,
they cordoned off the artwork's sea of porcelain
seeds, and threat of noxious dust motes, as would
any fear us Mongols and our horsemen.
Instead of wading through the work, the rub
of seeds against the shins – *each little member,*
each among the hordes, another schlub –
I thought, detached, of that inert September,
of Nisha Pillai in the early hours
ad-libbing over footage of the towers.

The planes impacting into steel sear
their image to the dark's imagination.
Conceptual art cannot at all compare
to it, so deft and cold in orchestration.
To dream it up, its vivid manifesto:
the first plane brought the news crews to the market,
the second a magician's flash, and presto
quiet to ourselves we said, 'Good target.'
The corporate heart of wealth, the miracle
America erected, bubble-wrapped
in brutalism: no empirical
mindset denies that 'blameless' is inapt.
But whispered, lest our ears misunderstand
and think we deem bin Laden's sculpture grand.

Conceptual art is tainted by the sheik's
set piece. And architecture too. The deed will
live in folklore longer than the blunt mistakes
that followed in response. It's his cathedral,
half-made like Gaudí's grand basilica
of holy folly, as indelibly
affecting, primary with blood's acrylic. The
escaping suicides from zealotry
and fire rained like fish, and Nisha Pillai
tried to summarise. I watched, was high,
and noodled with my pen, considered: 'Will I?
Sum up an act that suffers no reply?
In verse?' I could've. Poems are benign,
till Erdoğan kills thousands with a line.

Truth

i.
That everyone should be an atheist
is one of the beliefs ascribed, in fact
fallaciously, to atheism. Backed
by habit we connect a faith with this
assurance of its universal good,
this certainty that every fool should think
as we do. Or it feels safe to link
the truth with self-improvement, and it would
seem generous to share that betterment
with others. Atheism isn't though
essentially evangelistic. No,
the thought needs nothing as accelerant:
there are no gods. That's all. The point is brief.
It's light on what to do with that belief.

ii.
Additions that make sense to atheism
as a tenet are non-belief in similar
irreal constructs from beyond the singular,
embodied world: there is no wraith or lissom
soul transcending death; the narratives
of arcane origins religions of
the world dispense are myths, their fictions have
accreted into place; and then there are declaratives
of good and sin, the seeing of innate
contours, morality above desire,
harm, approval, care – and all the fire

of competing interests these create –
they too are common human error, phantoms,
the good of truth the lightest of the bantams.

iii.
Rebuttals will arise from humanists
at this, of throwing baby with its water
from the bath – truth's good with Christian thought – a
view I share. That I illumine this
progression using logic indicates
I value truth. But this is me, my flaw,
and not of truth itself, truth's goodness nor
the charm an infant mannequin creates
for truth. My values can't escape the snail's
slick of childhood psychology –
delusions of both fixed biology
and those transmitted virus-like on veils
of phrase and glance that countermand the brain.
No, heave the old bathwater in the drain.

During John Travolta's Face/Off Operation . . .

. . . they discovered he had 39 faces all stacked one on top of the other
for easy access.
Always another face underneath.
SLICE this one's Christian Slater SLICE here's Jeremy Irons SLICE
Margaret Thatcher, etc.
Who's your plastic surgeon? asked one of the face/off operators.
This is some intricate work.
John Travolta looked at the guy.
Regulation company jumpsuit. Nondescript.

Body-count fodder. Guy's gonna die for sure
and probably not in his own shot.
Probably three of these guys get wasted then the camera swings up
to the metal walkway.
Always a metal walkway in these places.
Guy's got a grey-blue jumpsuit and a blue-grey gloved hand
on the circular saw.
Not gonna see it coming.
Who's your plastic surgeon, Mr Travolta? Then BANG BANG BANG:

brains, guts, balls.
SLICE Darth Vader SLICE Freddy Mercury SLICE
Mr Miyagi out of *Karate Kid*.
Karate Kid 3 though. Trying to be professional but less you know fire.
John Travolta looked up at the walkway.
Where's that go? he asked the anaesthetist.
Fuck you, thought the anaesthetist. Just so fuck
completely you.
SLICE Little Mermaid SLICE Liberace SLICE White Fang SLICE

who's that?

That's you. Deep in the face stack.

Thought you were something, but no.

Another face in Travolta's deck of visages.

Just another cheap grin in John Travolta's club sandwich of faces.

It's like Alberto said.

Dr Alberto. You know.

Sorry, the anaesthetist. Name got cut due to run time.

You look like your mother.

Genetic Modification for Knee-Socked Underlings

The greatest thing that progress and endeavour
have unearthed that leaps, bounds, gads
and ever ups the apex of our clever
species's accomplishments is ads.
Grafitti's just our cheaper counterfeit.
Though if you're spry of heel enough to work
some slick and stitch the look or sound of it
to sitcom breaks, superb, please go bezerk
on it. But otherwise, a Vivid, cuz.
Let's worm into our nearest gents (or for
you few ungainly women, lab-light buzz
still frazzling your eyes, the other door)
and just above the roll jot proudly, say:
Back off you teen Pol Pots! GM OK!

iv. Louche and Vain

Five Recycled Single-Use Items

The urologist was surrounded by a bevy of average-looking eunuchs.

**

I have with me in my satchel, Your Honour, a shred of evidence.

**

Franky Knuckles had a close haircut, a close waxing of the hindquarters, but a distant shave.

**

You speak in dry tones tempered by a dulcet mouthful of semi-masticated caramels.

**

Both Hong and his wife were social caterpillars, liquefying in the party's cocoon.

Superman

Halfway up the ascent zigzagging
            from Royal Terrace
                        to upper Stuart Street carrying four too-heavy
            grocery bags I begin to understand

that I will not make it.
                My huffing personage –
                            from the fingers, white
            with the strain, to a face

the colour of rhubarb – will ooze
                into the pavement
                            and roll
            slowly down the hill

on what once was my back.
                I am lugging
                        groceries so as to cook for you.
            It's a pivotal meeting, cooking for you

for the first time, you a gastronome,
                but me now a gastropod, glossy
                        like a slug
            and unable to lift four ridiculous bags

with slug fingers
                any further up this mountain.
                        I own no food processor
            so have prearranged to meet you at a friend's.

Why did I not consider the logistics of the operation
               from gravity's belvedere:
                              ask to borrow the food processor,
          and schlep that instead

but downhill, perhaps sitting on it
               and riding it like a luge?
                              Because my head is fat.
          I take another step.

I don't have a cellphone.
               I cannot ring a taxi.
                              You will arrive in minutes and I have to be
          cooking. I take another step. Also

my flat is a pigpen
               with no table.
                              Another. This is how marathon runners feel
          when they give up.

This is how I should have felt when I gave up
               on my master's thesis after two years
                              but felt only freedom.
          If I just opened my hands

and let the bags drop.
               If I just let my face crumple into a sneer
                              and walk away, the flour,
          the feta, the whole block of butter

when a quarter of it would've sufficed
            spilling into the dark unnoticed,
                        I could feel the same sweet dereliction
      and liberty. Instead

I trudge another chicken-step upwards.
            No one will thank me.
                        No one will appreciate this when I recount it.
      But I will know.

For years this story will sting
            like lemon juice on a papercut
                  in the memory.
      I will try to chisel it into prose

and find it unsatisfactory, lacking
            in the requisite suffering.
                        I'll distil that to a sonnet, which will seem too
      clipped and grandiose.

In the meantime the steps have stopped.
            I am only at Moana Pool. Why
                  do my eyeballs ache?
      I try running. The running lasts less time

than can be considered definitional of the term.
            Centuries of half-seconds pass.
                        I have no feeling in my hands but
      here I am now on Stuart Street.

The plastic has not cut through to the bone.
          Why did I bring Grapetise as well as wine?
                    Choose one and be glad of it.
     No more memories form.

All energy is diverted to the legs.
          The mouth can hold no other expression
                    but a stroke-victim grimace.
     I shuffle around the back to the door.

I try not to make a big thing
          out of the horror of the ascent,
                    but later I marry you, and I know
     it's because I made this climb,

that I pushed out the strides, that
          I fought when my blood hissed
                    that there was no fight left to fight with.
     Everyone may say, So you carried some bags up a hill?

But they are all the scum children of the sewers
          and I am the husband who
                    made vol-au-vent, who
     staggered up a sheerness of the will

and surmounted it.

Kay? Syrah? Shiraz?

Orally, the Syrah slips
(and wakes up black along my lips).

Astride my point, with stirrups stuck,
I slurred and slurped its syrups up.

How louche and gauche.
How loose it goes;
my purple tongue
speaks weeks of prose.

So as to Fit Back into One's Bikini

You've tried it? Soy-dehydrated
sand-and-whispers
ice cream? You should.
Very good for starvation enabling, and
excellent on calcium, lime and rust.

**

Do only the doable, but think
the undoable.

**

The fortnights of summer blink
empty blue eyes.

**

The abyssal diet allows massive consumption!
Eat a canyon!
It is O the most vestal of clean eating,
the intaking of vistas.
Suck up a crater!
For more on crevasses and chasms
read my book.

**

When you stare, bored, into the abyss
the abyss yawns.

Slung Across the Cat

In the evenings, slung across the cat,
we watched TV.
It wasn't some rattling sound in the corner that we talked over,
passed into the room and out of,
stood in front of with our arses towards it
and our rabbit teeth caught in a sneer,
or drifted away from and forgot about.
We positioned ourselves across from the great wide screen
and studied it.
There were many species of things we sought out
in our channel-flipping
and booking-in.

Tension was an essential:
mortal tension, anxiety,
shrieked tension, sublimated tension,
irony.
It was the taboo we were seeking out.
It was irreverence,
culture-secret Tourette's.
We wanted the television to sting us with shock.
And what we saw in psychopathy and horror was a reminder of
our thinness and fragility,
a shin-splinting for the sedentary mind.
We remarked in the silences.

You favoured dialogue and its idealised theatre of
human utterance.
You favoured the swordplay of words,

artful circumlocutions divorced from the stagnating circles
that real human interaction stuttered in
like scumborne fly-legs.
I favoured the ease and economy of stylists and editors.
My eyes grazed light-handed production design,
the deft costumery and lighting, eating it
with a sloth's fingers.
We admired storytelling,
the tale well told,

the playing-off of genre,
and the well-rubbed routes of narrative headway,
the counterpoint,
the beauty of slick foreshadowing,
and the beauty of blunt foreshadowing.
We were moved by performance,
the fiction inhabited.
We were moved by the suffering,
the howling and tears and fury
or the stoical bearing of it.
The cat liked stillness and soporific mid-tones.
It affected tolerance.

Naked Analogue

'Warp! Warp!' a dog shielded behind its hedge commands.
'Visit a dizzy disc, Zig,' goes a cicada.

And back it all feeds into the gorse the wind of one's self-opinion
eddies through, disbanding on thorns and turbulence,
whispering tales of future grandeur, power.

'Heehaw,' a cat transmits, the path it floats up
glittering in crystals.

At first a droid then a Klingon, some tūī has
the frankness of the nonhuman we admire.
It is the shouting of vanity,

the confidence of adornment,
the straight-speaking of word chandeliers

and the ballet of beak that can be intricate, protracted,
but say only joy and desire.
It's silent, the sea, from here.

And its gull in the valley's air colonnade
threatens in a smear of distant white to pass out of

inaudibility, unwelcome sceptic, interrogating:
'Or?'
The sea is deep data. The ribbon of energy in the breakers

reports I am told via crabs and clams, gurgling
in the sand and imprinting into the salts I taste on the airstream,

the increments of change too slow and strong
to adequately synopsise.
Automating word noise from the stroller,

my son defines the wind in onomatopoeia:
'Zheesh!'

Then he spies the moon, our little naked analogue,
and tells the secret of its abased name.
'Zig zig zig,' the abridging cicada agrees.

Thy Wool Be Dun

Yes, it's dun coloured, my wool, thanks for noticing.
Once it was blonder, and thicker, and so gilded and ribbony that
more than one colleague bleated that it was Pre-Raphaelite.
I'm not making that up to create some desperate mystique
in my backstory, but I'm not saying the term wasn't at the time inapt.
But buffs and duns and beiges have their own honour.

v. Danny DeVito

Good Day, I Am a Horse

And hello, I am a beaver.
To you my sincerest, I am a starfish
with an old-fashioned disposition.
Ever yours, a beetle, one of many, writing,
amid a rainstorm, of commas, to an eagle.

Wotcher,

says I back,

an eagle, via telegraph (STOP).
Rustling in its seat, from back in the 1990s,
some undergraduate lofts its hand.
It drops it. It mutters the word
'anthropomorphisation' and wonders at a tut.

Get a grip, thinks a chorus

of skinks,

in French.
An extinct moa laughs in an extinct dialect
of Māori and slaps its beaked forehead.
A kitten on the internet holds up a sign:
Yoo iz so speshl hoominz haha.

Phrase Hack

As dry as ice.
  As wet as a whistle.
    As clean as a clergyman's clavicle.

Grayden depressed the receive-call button on his headpiece and yawned
his automated greeting:
'Welcome, hello, and can I or (why would I or) how can I help you?'

As Greek as to me all.
  As twice as the knock of how often the postman.
    As hotly as from off its tin roof the cat as anticipated.

Just as gain does, no gain involves a concomitant dollop of agony.
  No gain, pain.
If he wasn't the kind of depressing in a cheerleading outfit one offers
awareness-raising to he would tell it with pom-poms: pee aggressive, P-E
E-E-E
E-E-E-E
aggressive.

As cold as a baby's coffin.
  As soft as a cell.
    As clear as a jelly.

Grayden's mother, also called Grayden, worked at the bureau of
schadenfreude, sturm und angst, or births, deaths and marriages.
'It's me,' she retorted, hanging up on him.

As wide as a nun's garden.
As shaggy as a story of a dog in the 1970s.
As sweet as silk.

A Writer Wrongs

A hater hates
while a waiter waits.
A writer's wry
when the white-out's dry.

While you wander about MOMA or Noma
a little girl has to take a diploma.
(Modern wait staff are a perversity;
they need a paper at a technical university.)

A tomato, to mates,
is a passata as paste.
A potato mutates.
Two tostadas, to taste!

My waiter's waste.
My hater's haste.
So he's a little slapdash down
with a little flat hash brown.

So my fish is pallid.
So there's a little pebble in my freekeh salad.
Is it necessary a balladeer batters
out a ballad?

While I try to wangle my way into a comped meal
and fail, a waiter's patience frays.
While the squealers reel and the reelers squeal
a waiter weighs.

A writer longs
and a long wait angers.
A hater hates
and a writer panders.

A heater heats
a Rita Angus, seen
through the steam from the langoustine
with mangosteen.

And the wait's reprieve:
a writer's right
if a page is white
as a waiter's sleeve.

A Good Heart

for Dad

A good heart, a hurdler, no teeth in his mouth,
ping-pong, barl aboot, look, Stinker South.
Shining an apple, brushing the cinders,
calm then a panic: he's driving the Lindis.
The tour of the garden, currants black, currants red,
K-k-katie awaits, by the shine on the shed.
Hairdo like Einstein, or under his cap,
in cassock and alb for an afternoon nap.
An ice-cream-container-lid clerical collar,
a gentleman and a – one more time – scholar.
Phyll and her twin, Jean, Ben, Max and Daph.
I sent Dad some seeds, they were riffled by MAF.
Uncle Jack on piano, left and right handed,
Oh put your socks on! (The Eagle has landed.)
The hydro dam chaplain in a bright yellow parka,
second storey on Wye Street, whistling Tarka.
He goes to speak, pauses now, looks around, thinks;
on the slide and projector, he's next to the sphinx.
Egg flip and bicarb, the Ōmarama sky,
his boomerang rubber, three wet and three dry,
custard and mustard and pikelets and mince.
Watch out for the jug cord, Pete! It still makes him wince.
A joker, a card, here's his hernia scar.
That street's for bad eggs, don't get out of the car.
Kip with the Queen. Di marrying Geoff.
Talk to the left of him, the other ear's deaf.
Becca, gymnastic, Greg, face in a book,

the young woman's Carol, he makes her a Brook
on the steps of Columba, dark suit, looking dapper.
Why when I was a boy, a young whippersnapper.
Born on a table just five k away
from the room where he died. What is there to say?
The honourable member, Greg, Grandjim or Rev,
whoops he's flying an aeroplane, RNZAF.
Liz makes him a hot drink, Jennifer yells.
Feel the back of his hand, the dips and the swells.
As a priest he's a paragon, he's kind and he listens.
He drives half the day for the people he christens.
Stiff walk, Thousand Acre, fit for the heart of it,
TKS old man, dit dit-dah-dit dit.

The Brain

You can't just be built to tolerance. There has to be a buffer in case of more extreme phenomena. The organ of the skull is no different

to the one that pumps all the blood cells about. Could the aorta handle triple the work in a time of exceptional demand? Naturally. So to reveal the concealed depths of the brain's abilities, one must put it under stress.

Ionised

    emit

  gases   light of

      varying

        colours.

vi. Meat-Eating Breeders

I Coo Haiku High, Eh

for Ames

One Use a toothbrush, eh,   to clean your goose-
flesh ballbag,   then icewater it.

                                        The use?
Sweet fuck all.   Momentary relief, perhaps.
The itch, eternal.

                    Two Then Jesus claps:
Oi!   Throw no stones, you hypocrites!   (The king
of killjoys.)

                    Pilate's wife's repulsed.   A thing
so brutal. Why? Yet . . .   It's just so right now.

Three Always, we bring plagues: in the cacao,
minute mites;   moths, mice, flies and ants.
                                        How scabies
crazed me.   Like fleas that bite the baby's
brow, the unseen seethes.

                    Four His fluorescent
shite,   I scoop an iridescent   crescent
round his bits.

                    Am I infectious?   Are these
disease-borne fingers?   He wees, sighs: *Oh, please.*

Turn to Camera in the Birthing Suite

for Kate at 35

At this – *attaching a maternity*
pad's sticky wings to either side of your
gigantic knickers – I wink, turn to the
omniscient camera and say I'm sure
that none *submersed in postmodernity*
as deep as you have soared above their raw
and unrelievable eternity
of pain, fought unironic through the flaw
bonanza of the hypnobirth, the TENS
placebo and such taciturnity
or absence as the stand-in midwife lent,
and stayed so measured. I discern *indeed*
the greatest heroism in your labour.
And here's to Entonox to blunt the sabre.

Your Mother

i. Preeya

I need to wear a Cinderella dress.
It's after school. We're on the special sofa
where we air and solve things, though for
this catastrophe, I have to press
the point: I need to go to costume day
tomorrow in the dress. My monologue
gets tearful: I will never wear that frog
disguise again! Mum listens, says okay.
We beeline for the car, me at her hem,
and make it to the shop before it shuts.
She buys the fabric, makes a pattern, cuts
it out and has it sewn by 5am.
I wake to find my golden perfect raiment,
my friends who gag in jealousy, her payment.

ii. All the Marches

The autumns that incinerated by,
the 1980s dusk ablaze with pinks
and cherries in a phased Dunedin sky
or Adelaide's, the autumns as she slinks
around the lounge, her swaying perm so tall
and Whitney Houston gurgles from the hall.
Ayutthaya's hot seasons and the Wirral's
spring all burn with rain. We pass the murals
in the Metro – Michigan! The squirrels! –

and fight to numb a thought whose epidurals
find us in Morocco, just a hose
to wash with, though the Berbers smell of rose.
There's part of us still at the garden mall
with Whitney Houston playing to the sprawl.

Spring Is Sick with Child

Grey and morning-sick, spring
nurses itself like a pelican,
skimming a spoonbill of Cook Strait
ice water, and vomiting it back
onto Wellington in a trimester of rain.
The other seasons look on and quack
inanities. Summer coos from afar.
Summer blurts. Summer says of spring's

grey lump, you must be so happy.
Winter is unfiltered. Winter doesn't
want to dance on sugar-coated
eggshells. It wishes spring
to entertain no false hope: this
will get worse. Autumn mansplains
through its duck beard that spring
shouldn't be eating the Camembert.

Put it down it says, as heads turn.
Put it down, the only thing that
is bringing any comfort. The weeks
puke on. Spring's bud swells
inside it like a rolling wave of corn
and petals. It rains apple juice. It
rains pasta sauce. It rains yoghurt
and olive oil. The barometer stinks,

lurching in the wind, towards its eyrie,
a thrush's nest in a gutter's attic,

curry-hot, freezer-cold. Just colossally,
diarhoeally dreck: the outside is
the open souvlaki of a nappy in wait.
On the tin roof, a kākā retches
and tweets the season's headache.
Ice water. Grey, regurgitated rain.

Horodok: The Altar of the Reeds

after David Eggleton's translation of Georg Trakl

Amidst the trees, the twilit autumn shreds
the shelling's echo. Pasture burns to gold,
the lake to blue. Then dark and evening's reds
resume. As night wheels in and shadows hold
their mutilated mouths, they groan, the soldiers,
seeping in the bogs their clouds of blood.
A killer swims the swamp, whose touch is cold as
moonlight: whimpers bubble in the mud
and fade, or linger on to live and rot
beneath a golden canopy of swaying
stars. The troop of corpses stand, unknot
their limbs and wipe their headwounds, all arraying
to salute the god among the reeds
who feeds on pain. Their grandsons' too she needs.

Kid in Day Care, Cat Sleeps in Pram

Where is my tormentor now? I miss his tiny pincer
fingers. This perambulating lookout reeks of his
outpourings. Recall I have never pierced his skin with my

slashers. I have never bitten him even as a warning.
Recall I bite and slash all creatures, every lumbering
goon that fills my saucer with gravy and sinew, every

hand that eases an itch or caresses a scent pad, every
roll on ecstasy
visitor whose shoes I   in   I cut them up.

I make shapes in blood in their wrists they fear will be
misinterpreted as self-harm. I sink my fangs artery-deep
in the incarnadine pulsations of human living. Skinks and

cicadas I behead. Native birds lie squirming and broken
under my neck fat. But some inner hunger tells me to
forsake the surgery on my brother-thing. Some sharp

avenues in my breeding that dodged cul-de-sacs and
manholes are shimmering, muting my teeth, sheathing
my barbs. Recall he totters onto me, his bulk enough to

pop my ribs, that he grips my tail, snatches hunks
from my fur, stabs my ears and eyes and stones me with
metal and wood, plastic and card. Into the basket I have

colonised he hurls terrifyingly empty spheres, singing
with static and the stench of rubber. I am paralysed by
his screeching. If I try to doze, he runs at me screeching,

arms a-flap. Up here, uncomfortable and comfortable on
crumbs and cushions and buckles, you must appreciate
the iconic countenance of my self-abnegation.

Acknowledgements

This book is for my son Ames, who I can only hope never reads it.

Thanks to the people, magazines, anthologies and websites that published these poems first: *Landfall* ('Art Is Weak' and 'A Writer Wrongs'), *Soft Cartel* ('During John Travolta's Face/Off Operation . . .', 'Good Day, I Am a Horse', 'I Coo Haiku High, Eh' and 'Turn to Camera in the Birthing Suite'), *Queen Mob's Teahouse* ('Five Recycled Single-Use Items', 'Five Ways I Would End a Sonnet on Shelley's Cremation', 'No More Experimental Poetry', 'Selfie, Dumfries, 1998' and 'Spring Is Sick with Child'), *The Spinoff* ('Gone Mad' and 'Superman'), *St Luke's Oamaru Parish Magazine* ('A Good Heart'), *Deep South* ('Kay? Syrah? Shiraz?'), *Turbine | Kapohau* ('Phrase Hack' and 'Truth'), *New Zealand Poetry Shelf* ('Slung Across the Cat' – audio), *Brief* ('Wellington Zoo 44 Rewritten'), and in *Dandy Bogan: Selected Poems*, Boatwhistle, 2018 ('The Brain', 'Self-Planting of Evidence' and 'Your Mother').

Colossal thanks to those who have supported my writing, whether through encouragement, feedback or eye-rolling, both on social media and, by the depressing number of luddites I seem to know, not: Cilla McQueen, Michael Steven, Richard Reeve, David Karena-Holmes, Blair Reeve, Katherine Dolan, John Dolan, Rob Allan, Kay McKenzie Cooke, Kylie Klein-Nixon, Steve Braunias, Pip Adam, Andy Paterson, Jim McNaughton, Simon Laube, Michelle Wanwimolruk, Erik Kennedy, Tren Wallis, Chris Tse, Bill Nelson, Harry Ricketts, Anna Jackson and Hamish Ironside. You too, person I've forgotten.

Thanks O peerless VUP – Ashleigh, Fergus, Therese, Kirsten, Craig. I cringe before you like a worm. Thanks to David Eggleton and David Beach for tolerating my reimagining of your work.

Thanks especially to Kate Wanwimolruk, who, despite making the grave mistake of marrying a poet, continues to be fathomlessly supportive in my writing. Many curtseys.